Rain Forest Homes

by Althea

illustrated by John Boyd Brent

Cambridge University Press

Cambridge
London   New York   New Rochelle
Melbourne   Sydney

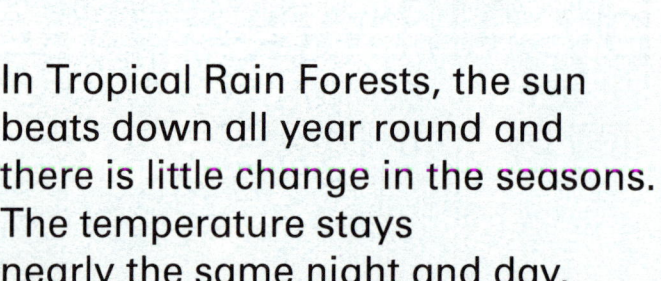

In Tropical Rain Forests, the sun
beats down all year round and
there is little change in the seasons.
The temperature stays
nearly the same night and day.

Most of the trees grow to a great height.
Their branches open out at the top
like umbrellas, to let the leaves and
flowers get light from the sun.
This canopy of leaves and branches
stops the light from reaching the ground.

Other plants struggle to reach
the light too. Vines climb
up around the trees and into
the top canopy.

When it rains it pours down in heavy drops.
Many of the leaves have a tip like
the spout of a jug which lets
the water drip to the ground.

There is so much rain that
it washes the goodness from the soil.
The soil is shallow, so
the trees can't grow long deep roots.
Instead they must grow
huge buttress roots to help
support their great height.

Seeds of ferns and orchids begin to grow
in gaps in the bark of trees.
Gradually they grow towards the light.
These ferns and orchids hang
from the enormous trunks,
providing homes for many insects.

Except near rivers or the edge of the forest it is always semi-dark on the forest floor. Few green plants can survive. Fungi don't need light to grow, so many spring up through the thick layer of wet rotting leaves which have dropped from the trees. The old leaves fall as new green leaves grow to replace them.

Beetles, ants and termites live here feeding on the rotting leaves, or each other.

The Giant Anteater uses its
strong claws to dig out ant and termite nests.
Its long snout and sticky tongue
will reach deep into the nests.
It licks up about 30,000 insects a day!
The Armadillo enjoys a meal of ants, too.

As well as running fast,
Jaguars will also climb trees or
swim to try and catch their prey.
They sit by streams catching fish with their paws
and waiting to pounce on other animals
when they come for a drink.

The Jaguar will sometimes risk attacking the Giant Anteater, but it usually hunts Tapir and other less strong mammals.

Tapirs like water and will wallow in the mud to try and get rid of the insects which live on them.

Many animals never come down to
the ground but live all their lives in
the top canopy of the forest.
The Sloth lives high up in the trees and
does everything upside down.
It feeds on fruit and leaves and even
sleeps while hanging by its feet from
the branches. Even its fur grows
in the opposite direction to other animals
so the rain can drip off easily.

It moves its stiff, rod-like legs
very slowly along the branches.
Luckily it is well camouflaged —
it even has green algae growing on its fur.
The caterpillars of a moth feed
on the algae.

The male Howler Monkey's roar
can be heard for several miles.
It warns other groups of
Howler Monkeys to keep away
from where his group is feeding.

Squirrel Monkeys leap from
tree to tree; their tails
help them to keep their balance.

The canopies of the forests are full of colourful birds, butterflies and even frogs. Blue and Yellow Macaws fly above the forest canopy, coming down to feed on fruit from the trees.

The Arrow Poison Frog carries
her tadpoles, one at a time, on her back
as she climbs through the canopy.
She searches for a small pool of water
in the base of a leaf, in which her tadpole can swim.

Huge Mahogany and Ebony trees grow side by side with Cola-nut trees. These nuts are used in making cola drinks.

Chimpanzees chatter noisily to one another as they feed and play. Gorillas and Chimpanzees feed on the ground and up in the trees, living in family groups. The older look after the young and keep them in order – slapping a youngster quite hard if it is very naughty.

Gorillas and Chimpanzees both have a rest in the middle of the day, sleeping in nests which they build in branches of trees.

Leopards will sometimes attack a young Gorilla or Chimpanzee.

Many animals grow very large
in the big, hot rain forests.
A Centipede, five times as large as
we normally see, comes out at night
in search of insects and worms.
It will even attack tiny lizards and frogs.
When the female lays her eggs
she curls round them to keep them
safe until they hatch.

Little is known about the life history
and foodplants of this rare
African Giant Swallowtail butterfly.
Its wings are 25 centimetres (10 ins)
across and its body contains enough
poison to kill six cats!

Centipede

Instead of swinging or leaping from tree to tree, some animals glide. The Flying Lemur, called the Colugo, has developed a wing-like skin which stretches from its front legs to its tail. It can glide up to 135 metres (443 feet). The Flying Frog glides, using its huge webbed feet as wings.
There is also a Flying Lizard and even a Gliding Snake!

Colugo

Flying Frog

Flying Fox

Gliding Snake

Many Bats live in rain forests too. Some feed on fruit, and have to climb among branches to find it.
The Flying Fox is the largest fruit-eating bat, measuring up to 1.5 metres (5 feet) across its wings when flying.

Hornbills have large beaks
and long eyelashes!
Except during the breeding season
they live together in large noisy
flocks, feeding on fruit and nuts.

They nest in holes in trees.
To keep the eggs and later the young
safe, the male helps the female to
seal herself into the nest by
closing up the entrance with clay
and her droppings.
They leave a narrow slit so he can
pass food to her while she
hatches the eggs.

Sadly, many rain forests, which have taken
thousands of years to grow, are being cut down
to make room for more farming land.
But the soil is not rich enough
to support many crops.
In other places the trees are being
cut to be used as timber and to make paper.

Scientists now think that much of the land may well become flooded if all the rain forests are cut down. At the moment the growing trees work like gigantic sponges, soaking up the heavy rain which falls on them.

Glossary

algae	simple plants usually living in water
buttress	something which supports something else. A buttress root spreads out from the trunk of a tree and helps support it.
camouflage	protective colouring to blend into surroundings
canopy	the layer of leaves and branches of trees above the forest floor
mammal	a warm blooded furry animal, which gives birth to live young which the female feeds on her own milk
Tropics, tropical	the Tropics are either side of the equator, between Cancer and Capricorn. Tropical Rain Forests are found in the Tropics